SUPER!!!!
DAD
JOKES

SAVING THE WORLD, ONE BAD JOKE AT A TIME

JIMMY NIRO

sourcebooks

Published by Sourcebooks
P.O. Box 4410, Naperville, Illinois 60567-4410
(630) 961-3900
sourcebooks.com

Printed and bound in the United States of America.
VP 10 9 8 7 6 5 4 3 2 1

TABLE OF CONTENTS

INTRODUCTION

Q: What is a **superhero**'s favorite drink?
A: Fruit **punch**.

There's no one as super as Dad—super silly, super weird, and super embarrassing. Celebrating the unsung humor and heroics of rad dads everywhere, this ultimate collection is packed with corny, literal, and ridiculous jokes on topics from sports and nature to food and entertainment and everything in between. But you don't have to be a dad to tell dad jokes, so put on your cape and save the world, one magnificently bad joke at a time!

If I could be any superhero, I think I'd be **Aluminum** Man so I could **foil** crime.

TOTAL TOMFOOLERY

I think **6:30** is the best time on the clock, **hands down**.

My dad once told me that if I wanted to make a difference in the world, I should put my **money** where my mouth is. He was right. I can really taste the **change**.

Q: What's the difference between a **b**ad joke and a **d**ad joke?
A: The **first letter**.

Lately, people have been making **apocalypse** jokes like there's **no tomorrow**.

· ⚡ ·

"Dad, why are you standing outside?"

"So if anyone asks, I'm **outstanding**."

· ⚡ ·

I don't always tell dad jokes, but when I do, he laughs.

· ⚡ ·

Q: What's yellow and kills you if you get it in your eye?
A: A bulldozer.

· ⚡ ·

Bad puns, that's how **eye roll**.

In a recent poll, 80 percent of people in America said they would not open their homes to a sentient **water basin** that walked up to their door and asked for shelter. Let that **sink** in.

"Dad, will you be coming to the **baby** shower?"

"I'd prefer a **full-size** shower, thanks."

Q: What superpower do you get when you become a **parent**?
A: Supervision.

I was really bored, so I made a **belt** out of all my watches. It was a **waist** of time.

I have this bad habit of kicking ice cubes under the refrigerator when they fall on the floor. One time, my wife caught me doing it and got really angry. She said I wasn't being responsible. A few hours later, though, she wasn't mad at me anymore. I guess it's all **water under the fridge**.

Q: Do you know what the leading cause of **dry skin** is?
A: Towels.

Q: What did the **windmill** say when she met her favorite celebrity?
A: "Oh my god! I'm such a **big fan!**"

I used to be addicted to the **hokeypokey**, but then I **turned myself around**.

Some people think my dad jokes are **childish**, which is crazy. They are obviously **full groan**.

"Dad, your jokes are hilarious. I think I have your sense of humor."

"Well, give it back!"

········

One time, I won a sweepstakes where the grand prize was a **one-year supply** of calendars. They only sent me one calendar.

········

Q: What did the **ghost** say when he introduced his girlfriend to his parents?
A: "This is my **boo**."

········

I feel bad for **Bigfoot**. He must have so much trouble finding **shoes** that fit.

"Did you know that all the people who live around here aren't allowed to be buried in the nearest cemetery?"

"Really? Why not?"

"Because they're still alive!"

My partner does a really great job **ironing**. I'm always im**pressed**.

Q: What's blue and smells like red paint?
A: Blue paint.

The **furniture** store keeps calling me, but I only wanted one **nightstand**!

Q: Why did the old lady fall down the well?
A: She didn't see that well.

- -

"Dad! Leave me a**lone**!"

"Okay, **how much** do you want?"

- -

Today, my son came downstairs and said, "Hey, do you have a bookmark?" I burst into tears. He's fourteen years old and still calls me "Hey" instead of "Dad."

- -

I'm like the **fabric** version of King Midas.
Everything I touch becomes **felt**.

- -

Q: What happened to the teenager who went to **jail**?
A: His face **broke out**.

They just opened a new store down the block. It's called **Moderation**. They have **everything in** there.

····························· ⚡ ·····························

Q: What does a house **wear**?
A: Ad**dress**.

····························· ⚡ ·····························

I told your mom that she had drawn her **eyebrows too high**. She **looked surprised**.

····························· ⚡ ·····························

Q: What do you call a story where everyone dies at the **end**?
A: A **dead end**.

····························· ⚡ ·····························

A banker told me that with the right savings account, I could **make money** off my money. It was **interest**ing.

I know I tell a lot of **knock knock** jokes, but I just a**door** them.

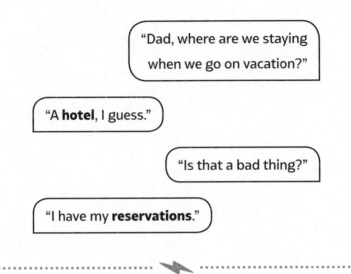

"Dad, where are we staying when we go on vacation?"

"A **hotel**, I guess."

"Is that a bad thing?"

"I have my **reservations**."

My wife and I were buying a new house, so she asked me to pick out a new **vacuum** cleaner. When I asked if she had any preferences about the choice, she said I should read some reviews of the vacuums that were available in our price range.

"I don't need to read reviews," I told her. "I already know they all **suck**."

If I had a **dime** for every book I've ever read, I would say, "Wow, what a **coin**cidence!"

"I think I have something in my shoe."

"I'm pretty sure that's a foot."

⚡

I keep trying to lose weight, but it keeps finding me.

⚡

Did you hear about the **invisible** man who married the invisible woman? I guess their kids weren't much to **look** at.

⚡

Q: What do **prisoners** use to call each other?
A: **Cell** phones.

⚡

I tried to have a conversation with my roommate when she was applying a **mud** mask. You should have seen the **filthy** look she gave me.

Q: What do you call an old person with really good **hearing**?

A: **Deaf** defying.

.... ⚡ ....

As I handed my dad his **fiftieth** birthday card, he looked at me with tears in his eyes and said, "You know, **one** would have been enough."

.... ⚡ ....

I can't stand **elevators**. They drive me **up the wall**.

.... ⚡ ....

My son must have been relieved to have finally been born. He looked like he was running out of **womb** in there.

.... ⚡ ....

Q: Why are **skeletons** so calm?

A: Nothing gets under their **skin**.

I woke up in the **fireplace** this morning. I guess you could say I slept like a **log**.

.... ➤ ....

Atheism is a non-**prophet** organization.

.... ➤ ....

"Dad, where's the **bin**?"

"I don't know. I haven't **been** anywhere!"

.... ➤ ....

I seem to have lost my **mood** ring. I'm not sure how I **feel** about it.

.... ➤ ....

Q: Why did the **picture** go to jail?
A: It was **framed**!

I traded our bed for a **trampoline**.
My spouse **hit the roof**.

Q: Why is your nose in the **middle** of your face?
A: It's the s**center**.

.... ➤ ....

My cell phone doesn't work in the **graveyard**.
I guess you could call it a **dead** zone.

.... ➤ ....

To the person on crutches who stole my **camouflage**
jacket: you can **hide**, but you can't run.

.... ➤ ....

I once met a man who had **five** legs. His pants fit
like a **glove**.

.... ➤ ....

The **skeleton** never gives his friends any valentines.
His **heart** just isn't in it.

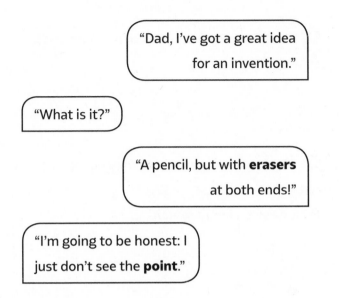

"Dad, I've got a great idea for an invention."

"What is it?"

"A pencil, but with **erasers** at both ends!"

"I'm going to be honest: I just don't see the **point**."

Once upon a time, a man found a magic lamp in a cave. When he rubbed the lamp, a genie came out.

"Hello!" said the genie. "I have the power to grant you three wishes. What's your first wish?"

The man couldn't believe his luck. He thought for a moment, then said the first thing that came into his mind.

"I wish I were rich," the man said.

The genie nodded and snapped his fingers to make it so.

Then he said, "Done. What's your second wish, Rich?"

Q: What do you call a man with a **rubber toe**?
A: Roberto.

· ⚡ ·

Q: Why was the **borrowed money** happy to be returned?
A: It wasn't a **loan** anymore.

· ⚡ ·

I used to be addicted to not **showering**, but I eventually got **clean**.

· ⚡ ·

"Dad, you haven't listened to a single word I've said, have you?"

"Whoa! That's an odd way to start a conversation with me."

A company is introducing glass **coffins**. Will they be successful? **Remains** to be seen.

······································ ⚡ ······································

My grandpa was a great man. I'll always remember the last thing he said to me before he kicked the bucket.

He said, "How far do you think I could kick this bucket?"

······································ ⚡ ······································

My best friend's name is **Clarence**. I like him because he always has the best **sales**.

······································ ⚡ ······································

You can never believe a **chair** that talks about **cotton**. It's **full of it**.

······································ ⚡ ······································

Q: What do you call a person who hates **pencils**?
A: An **erac**ist.

Have I told you my story about **screws, nuts**, and **bolts**? Most people say it's **rivet**ing.

Last night at dinner, I told a great joke about **undelivered** mail. Unfortunately, nobody seemed to **get it**.

All my friends have such extensive **bucket** lists. Mine seems a little **pail** in comparison.

This year, to raise tax revenues, the government is instituting a **garbage bag** tax. There's been a lot of debate about it. On one side, people think it's too **Hefty**, while other people are **Glad**. My local news station interviewed me and asked what I thought.

I commented, "Honestly, I think the whole thing is **trash**."

The **calendar** had better watch its back. Its **days are numbered**.

.... ➤➤ ....

"Dad, I don't want to go visit Grandma and Grandpa. They're kind of boring."

"Well, that's a rude thing to say. You at least have to admit that their **chairs** are **rockin'**."

.... ➤➤ ....

I decided to sell our **vacuum** cleaner. It was just **gathering dust**.

.... ➤➤ ....

Sometimes, my friends don't believe I'm **Jewish**. When I tell them, they say, "No way!" and I just respond, "**Yahweh**."

Q: What did the **flame** tell his parents when he fell in love?

A: "I've found the perfect **match**!"

My wife said it was a waste of money to buy a four-foot-wide **frame** for our wedding photo, but I think she should look at the **bigger picture**.

I just read a book about **Japanese warriors**. It was a little long, but I can **samurais** it for you.

Q: Why did George Washington have so much trouble **sleeping**?

A: He couldn't **lie**.

Let me tell you: nostalgia ain't what it used to be.

I'm thinking of getting a new **haircut**, but I need to **mullet** over.

I was going to make a joke about **banking**, but I can't think of one **atm**.

Dad, I found some **change** in your pants pocket when I was doing the laundry.

"Are you telling me that you **laundered money**?"

I got a letter the other day saying my tax return was outstanding. It was nice to get a compliment from the IRS, but I honestly can't remember submitting my taxes.

Q: What do you call a snobby criminal going down the stairs?

A: A condescending con descending.

Q: When is a **door** not a door?

A: When it's **ajar**.

Last Saturday night, I was having a good time when a **bouncer** approached me and asked me to leave.

"Why?" I asked him. "I haven't done anything wrong!"

"Well," the bouncer said, "I have no idea who you are, and this is my **trampoline**."

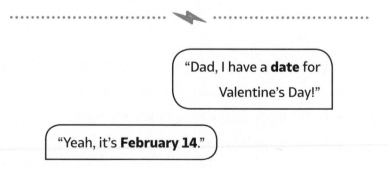

"Dad, I have a **date** for Valentine's Day!"

"Yeah, it's **February 14**."

THE GRIN OUTDOORS

I won an argument with a weather **forecaster** once. His logic was **cloudy**.

.... ➤ ....

Q: How do **trees** communicate with one another?
A: They **bark**.

.... ➤ ....

I asked my astronomy teacher to explain what an **eclipse** was, but she left me in the **dark**.

"Dad, I got a bad **sun**burn at the beach today."

"That's impossible. You can only get a **daughter**burn!"

Q: What did the **ocean** say to the shore?
A: Nothing. It just **wave**d.

Q: What do you call a collage of **pictures** of all different types of plants?
A: **Photo**synthesis.

When I was a kid, my neighbors hired me to clean up the **leaves** in their yard. For a week or so, I was really **raking** it in.

Q: What do you call a **tree** that does science experiments?
A: Chemis**tree**.

· ➤ ·

They keep saying that money doesn't grow on **trees**, but then why do banks have **branches**?

· ➤ ·

"It's really **mug**gy out today."

"I just looked out the window, and I didn't see any **mugs**."

· ➤ ·

When **spring** finally arrives, I get so excited that I wet my **plants**.

Q: Have you ever heard the joke about the three **holes in the ground**?
A: Well, well, well.

My wife says I'm too obsessed with **astronomy**. What **planet** is she on?

Q: How much space do **fungi** need to grow?
A: As **mushroom** as possible.

"What did you learn about in school today?"

"Outer **space**."

"You're a bit young for that. Did it go **over your head**?"

Q: What kind of flower grows on your **face**?
A: Tulips.

The sun doesn't need to go to **college**. It already has twenty-eight million **degrees**.

Q: How did the **tree** stay in shape?
A: He did **planks**.

I used to get **sea**sickness all the time, but now it comes in **waves**.

Q: What type of shorts do **clouds** wear?
A: Thunderwear.

Have I told you about **gravity**? It's very **down to earth**.

Q: How does the **moon** cut his hair?
A: Eclipse it.

- ➤ -

Q: What is the **smartest** mountain?
A: Mount **Clever**est.

- ➤ -

"Dad, how many **feet** are in a yard?"

"It depends on how many **people** are standing in it."

- ➤ -

Weather reporting is **snow** joke. I take my job very **cirrus**ly.

- ➤ -

Q: What did the outraged **flower** say?
A: "What in **carnation**?"

I hate debating in **space**. My arguments don't carry any **weight.**

.... ➤ ....

Q: What did the plant say when it was **hungry**?
A: "I could use a **light** snack."

.... ➤ ....

"Dad, do you like the **flowers** I planted?"

"They're **growing** on me."

.... ➤ ....

Q: Why did the **ocean** break up with its significant other?
A: It didn't want to be **tide** down.

.... ➤ ....

What do you call the **sticky stuff** inside trees? I need to know A**SAP.**

ANIMALS & HORSEPLAY

Q: Did you hear about the **buffalo** that lived two hundred years?

A: It just celebrated its **bison**-tennial.

Q: What do you call a lazy baby **kangaroo**?

A: A **pouch** potato.

Elephants must hate running on the beach. They just can't keep their **trunks** up.

Q: What do you call an **owl** that does magic tricks?

A: Hoodini.

Q: Why did the **octopus** beat the shark in a fight?
A: He was well **armed**.

.... ➤ ....

I wrote a book about **birds** once. My publisher said it **flew** off the shelves!

.... ➤ ....

Q: Why did the **giraffe** break up with her boyfriend?
A: He was a **cheetah**.

.... ➤ ....

"Dad, what animal can jump higher than a house?"

"All of them. Houses can't jump!"

Q: What did the **llama** say when he was invited to a picnic?

A: "Great! **Alpaca** lunch."

························ ➤ ························

Q: What did the **beaver** say when he ran into a wall?

A: "**Dam**!"

························ ➤ ························

Hey, do you need to build an **ark**? Because I **Noah** guy.

························ ➤ ························

Q: What do you call a fish with no **eyes**?

A: A fsh.

························ ➤ ························

Q: Which animal has even more lives than a cat?

A: A **frog**; it **croaks** every night.

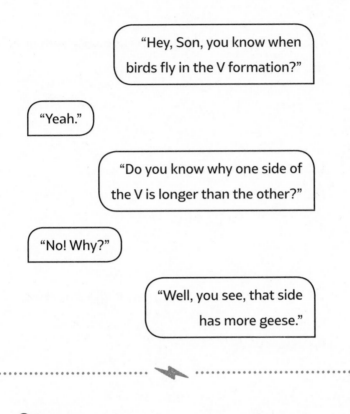

"Hey, Son, you know when birds fly in the V formation?"

"Yeah."

"Do you know why one side of the V is longer than the other?"

"No! Why?"

"Well, you see, that side has more geese."

Q: What's **orange** and sounds like a parrot?
A: A **carrot**.

Q: What do you call an **elephant** that doesn't matter?
A: An irr**elephant**.

The police arrested a **dog** that was giving birth on the side of the road. She was **litter**ing.

Q: What do you call a fly without wings?
A: A walk.

Q: What game do **chickens** play in the swimming pool?
A: Marco **Pollo**.

Dolphins are weird animals. Seriously, what **porpoise** do they serve?

Q: What do you call an explosive **horse**?
A: **Neigh**-palm.

Q: What do you call an alligator in a **vest**?

A: An in**vest**igator.

Q: What kind of cow is hairy on both the inside and the outside?

A: The kind that's standing in the doorway of the barn.

My **cat** just got sick on the carpet. I don't think she's **feline** well.

Q: What is a **kangaroo**'s favorite thing about beer?

A: The **hops**.

Q: How do you make an octopus **laugh**?

A: With its ten**tickles**.

Q: What happens when you stand between two **llamas**?

A: You get **llama**nated.

Q: How do you tell the difference between an alligator and a crocodile?

A: You'll see one later and the other in a while.

Have you heard about the pregnant **bed** bug? She's going to have her babies in the **spring**.

Q: What type of magazines do **cows** read?

A: **Cattle**logs.

Q: Why are **cats** such bad storytellers?

A: They only have one **tale**.

I was going to tell a joke about a golden **retriever**, but it seemed a tad far-**fetched**.

Someone has been stealing **dogs** in our
neighborhood. The police said they have
several **leads**.

. . . . ➤ . . . .

Q: What do you call a bear who's lost all his **teeth**?
A: A **gummy** bear.

. . . . ➤ . . . .

Q: What do you call a **horse** that moves around a lot?
A: Un**stable**.

. . . . ➤ . . . .

I saw a **spider** in my house the other day. As I was going to
squish it, my friend stopped me.

"No, don't kill it!" she exclaimed. "Take it out instead."

So we went out for drinks. He was a neat guy. It seemed
like he wanted to be a **web designer**.

Q: What do you call a pile of **cats**?
A: A **meow**ntain.

························➤························

Q: Why couldn't the animals on Noah's Ark play **cards** to pass the time?
A: Noah was standing on the **deck**.

························➤························

I **spotted** a jaguar today. Now it looks like a **leopard**.

························➤························

Q: Why aren't dogs good dancers?
A: They have two left feet.

························➤························

Q: What do you call a **shy** bee?
A: A **mumble**bee.

Q: Why do **cows** have hooves and not feet?

A: Because they **lactose**.

.... ➤ ....

One time, I was driving with my dad. We were going down the highway on a hot summer day. Suddenly, a big bug flew out of nowhere and hit our windshield with a **splat**. My dad was nonplussed.

"I bet he wouldn't have the **guts** to do that again."

.... ➤ ....

Q: Why should you never count your money while standing on an **anthill**?

A: You might fin**ance** in your pants.

.... ➤ ....

Q: What did the **buffalo** say the day his son left for college?

A: "**Bison**."

I named my **horse** Mayo. Mayo **neighs**.

.... ➤ ....

Q: What do you call a cow that has been **knighted**?
A: Sirloin.

.... ➤ ....

Q: What do you call a dog that does **magic** tricks?
A: A la**bracadabra**dor.

CLASS CLOWN

What do you get when you cross a joke with a rhetorical question?

Q: What do you call a **lesson** about turtles?
A: A **turtorial**.

I almost went to **astronaut** school as a kid, but when my parents tried to enroll me, we found out they were **outer space**.

Q: Why was **Karl Marx** teased by his classmates in school?

A: He couldn't **capitalize**.

"Mom says **curse** words are bad. Do you ever curse, Dad?"

"Of course not. I **swear**!"

I didn't graduate ninja school, but only because no one ever knew I was in the class.

Q: What is a **witch**'s favorite subject in school?

A: Spelling.

My teacher says that **fish** are more intelligent than we give them credit for. They spend a lot of time in **schools**.

I was on a college tour with my daughter the other day. Walking past the engineering building, the tour guide told us that the engineering program was revered but very difficult to get into. So I tried the door.

I responded, "Nah, it's unlocked, and the door isn't that heavy."

. . . . ⚡ . . . .

I don't believe in "*i* before *e* except after *c*." It's been disproved by s**cie**nce.

. . . . ⚡ . . . .

"Did you know there was a kid**napping** at your school today?"

"What? No!"

"It's okay. He **woke** up."

Q: What did the **notebook** say when it graduated?
A: "**College ruled**."

I once skipped school to go **bungee** jumping with my friends. We got **suspended**.

Q: What did the **pirate**'s report card look like?
A: He always got **seven Cs**.

Culinary school is easy. The final exam is a piece of **cake**!

I come from the school of hard **knocks**. That's why I don't use **doorbells**.

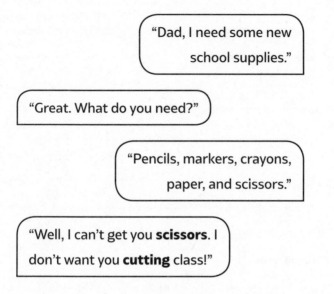

"Dad, I need some new school supplies."

"Great. What do you need?"

"Pencils, markers, crayons, paper, and scissors."

"Well, I can't get you **scissors**. I don't want you **cutting** class!"

Did you hear about the boy who went to **mime** school? He was never **heard** from again.

Q: What word is always spelled wrong?
A: *Wrong.*

I just invented an awesome new word: plagiarism.

I'll never date an **apostrophe** again. The last one was too **possessive**.

.... ⚡ ....

I was shopping in a bookstore and couldn't find what I was looking for.

"Can I help you, sir?" the shopkeeper asked.

"Sure," I said. "Can you help me find a play by Shakespeare?"

"Of course!" the shopkeeper said. "Which one?"

"Oh," I said, surprised he didn't know. "William."

.... ⚡ ....

I thought I was doing well in **gym** class, but I ended up with a B. They must have been using **weight**ed grades.

.... ⚡ ....

Q: What can you say to comfort someone who is a stickler for **grammar**?

A: "**There, their, they're.**"

I just finished reading a book about **Stockholm syndrome**. It was awful at first, but **by the end**, I kind of loved it.

.... ➤ ....

> "Dad, I need help with my grammar homework. Can you name **two pronouns**?"

> "**Who**, **me**?"

.... ➤ ....

I got carried away playing **Scrabble** last night and swallowed a handful of tiles. I'm worried that could **spell** disaster.

.... ➤ ....

Q: What's the best way to talk to a **giant**?
A: Use **big** words.

I was at a friend's funeral, and his widow asked me to say a word about him.

I hadn't prepared anything, so I just said the first thing that came into my mind, "**Plethora**."

Fortunately, the widow was moved. She said, "Thank you. That **means a lot**."

· ⚡ ·

On my first day of school, I signed up for English, math, science, and geography. The rest was history.

· ⚡ ·

Q: Why didn't Dracula get into **art** school?
A: He could only **draw** blood.

· ⚡ ·

I wasn't quite good enough to get into the prestigious **marionette** school, but I knew someone who could pull some **strings**.

You know what they say about kids who refuse to do their **math** homework? They never **amount** to anything.

Q: Why did **Neil Armstrong**'s son get suspended from school?

A: He was being **astronaught**y.

·· ⚡ ································

When I was in school, my **science** teacher always liked making puns. One day, when he was passing out papers for a pop quiz, he reminded us that cheating would not be tolerated and that we would surely be caught if we tried.

"I've got my **ion** you," he said.

·· ⚡ ································

A bank robber walked into a bank and pulled a gun.

"Okay everyone!" he yelled. "Give me all the money or you're **geography**!"

The bank tellers looked at each other confused. "Do you mean **history**?" one of them asked.

"Don't change the **subject**!" the robber yelled.

LOCATION, LOCATION, LOCATION

If we have a race around the world, it should end in **Europe**. That's the **Finnish** line.

··

If I were to **wander** around Italy, would I be **Roman**?

··

Q: Why is **Tel Aviv** a great place to vacation?
A: It **Israeli** fun.

I saw a beautiful tower in **Italy**. It was a **Pisa** art.

I went swimming in a river in **France**. My best friend went swimming in a river in **Egypt**. When we got home and compared stories about our travels, he said I was in**seine**. I told him he was in de**nile**.

Q: What did the Parisian man say when he **tripped**?
A: "Oh no! Eif**fel**!"

The restaurant burned my **Hawaiian** pizza last night. I told them they should have put the oven on **aloha** setting.

I heard on the news that someone had robbed the Tokyo **Origami** Museum in Japan. The anchor said that the story was still **unfolding**.

.... ⚡ ....

Q: Why is it hard for someone from the **South Pacific** to sit still?
A: They are quite **Fiji**ty.

.... ⚡ ....

A travel agent told me he could get me a free trip to **Egypt** if I could get five other people to sign up too. It sounded like a **pyramid** scheme.

.... ⚡ ....

Q: Why is the **Czech Republic** so sensible?
A: Because everyone is very **Prague**matic.

Don't you hate jokes about **German sausages**? They're the **wurst**.

I applied for a job at a zoo in **Australia**, but they told me I wasn't **koala**fied.

.... ➤ ....

My best friend went to **the Middle East** for summer vacation. When she got back, she showed me some cool photos and told me about all the sites she'd seen.

I was wondering if she got any cool souvenirs, so I decided to ask, "**Dubai** anything?"

.... ➤ ....

Q: Where do most **superheroes** live?
A: **Cape** Town.

.... ➤ ....

Have you heard about the big **dental** convention they have in Nevada every year? I think it's called **Floss** Vegas.

Q: What do you call a hippie's **wife**?
A: Mississippi.

.... ⚡ ....

Some people don't believe in **Jesus**, but I think he **Israel**.

.... ⚡ ....

I hear the **pastries** in Italy are amazing. I **cannoli** imagine.

.... ⚡ ....

Q: What's the difference between an African elephant and an Indian elephant?
A: About five thousand miles.

.... ⚡ ....

Contrary to popular belief, the first french **fries** weren't actually cooked in France. They were cooked in **Greece**.

England doesn't have a **kidney** bank, but it does have a **Liver**pool.

No matter how kind you are, German **children** are **kinder**.

····························· ➤ ·····························

Q: How did **Swedish** people get so good at building furniture?
A: No **IKEA**!

····························· ➤ ·····························

Q: Why do **Norway**'s naval ships have barcodes on their hulls?
A: So when they come back, it's easy to **scan the navy in**.

····························· ➤ ·····························

I'm starting a new job in **Seoul** next week. It just seems like it will be a good **Korea** move.

····························· ➤ ·····························

Geology rocks, but **geography** is **where it's at**.

Q: Where did the **crayon** go for its summer vacation?
A: Colorado.

························ ➤ ·····················

I'd like to go to **Holland** someday, **wooden shoe**?

························ ➤ ·····················

Q: What did the **stamp** say to the letter?
A: "**Stick** with me, and you'll go places."

························ ➤ ·····················

Italian building inspectors in **Pisa** are **lean**ient.

GOURMET GAGS

A slice of apple pie is $2.50 in Jamaica and $3.00 in the Bahamas. These are the **pie rates** of the Caribbean.

I used to be addicted to Thanksgiving **leftovers**. I had to quit **cold turkey**.

Q: What is Santa's favorite **pizza**?
A: One that's **deep-pan, crisp, and even**.

I'm really worried about eating **salads** after this *E. coli* outbreak, but **lettuce romaine** calm.

· ➤ ·

Q: Why do Dasher and Dancer love **coffee**?
A: Because they're Santa's **star bucks**!

· ➤ ·

Q: What is the **sleepiest** fruit?
A: **Nap**ricot.

· ➤ ·

My wife hates it when I mess with her **red wine**. I added some fruit and orange juice—now she's **sangria** than ever.

· ➤ ·

Q: What does a **clock** do when it's hungry?
A: It goes back **four seconds**.

Did you hear about the criminal
who kept his **spices** in the freezer?
He served hard **thyme**.

Q: What do you call someone who is **obsessed** with bananas?
A: A ban**aniac**.

.... ⚡ ....

Did you hear the rumor about **butter**? No? Well, I'm not going to **spread** it around.

.... ⚡ ....

Q: Why did the police arrest the **turkey**?
A: They suspected **fowl** play.

.... ⚡ ....

Potato puns are a little tricky. You need to **stew** on them a little; you can't just **russet**.

.... ⚡ ....

Q: What did the **demon** eat for breakfast?
A: **Devil**ed eggs.

I got hit in the head with a can of **Pepsi** today, but don't worry. It was a **soft** drink.

.... ➤ ....

Q: What kind of tea do you drink with the **queen**?
A: **Royal**tea.

.... ➤ ....

I was out to lunch with some friends last week. I wasn't super hungry, so I decided just to order soup and salad.

When I told the server I wanted tomato soup and a Caesar salad, he said, "Great! For the soup, do you want a cup or a bowl?"

"That's probably a good idea," I said. "Otherwise, the soup will go all over the table!"

.... ➤ ....

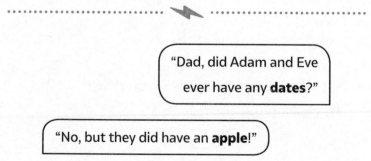

"Dad, did Adam and Eve ever have any **dates**?"

"No, but they did have an **apple**!"

Q: Why did the pilgrims' **pants** keep falling down during Thanksgiving dinner?

A: Because their **belt buckles** were on their hats.

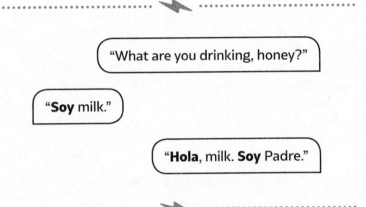

"What are you drinking, honey?"

"**Soy** milk."

"**Hola**, milk. **Soy** Padre."

My friends and I went out for breakfast last Sunday, and I ordered bacon and eggs.

"How do you like your eggs?" the server asked.

I was confused and responded, "I don't know. I haven't had them yet!"

People don't like bending over to get their drinks. We need to **raise the bar**.

Q: How does Moses make **coffee**?

A: He**brews** it.

Q: What did the **sushi** say to the bumblebee?
A: "**Wasabi**?"

.... ⚡ ....

I was watching the news the other day, and there was a big story about a **vegetable** cargo ship that sank in the Pacific Ocean. The news anchor said that after much investigation, researchers had determined what caused the ship to sink. It had too many **leeks**.

.... ⚡ ....

Q: Why did the **banana** put sunscreen on?
A: It was starting to **peel**.

.... ⚡ ....

Today I read about a man who got arrested for stealing bread. The police caught him **bread** handed.

Q: Why did the alien want to move out of the **Milk**y Way?
A: He was ga**lactose** intolerant.

······················· ➤ ·······················

When **nonstick cooking spray** went to school, her friends tried to nickname her **Pam**, but it just **didn't stick**.

······················· ➤ ·······················

"This isn't the burger I ordered! I asked for no pickles, and they still put a **pickle** on it!"

"Well, **dill** with it."

······················· ➤ ·······················

I dreamed about drowning in an ocean made out of **orange soda** last night. It was just a **Fanta** sea.

My wife first agreed to go on a date with me after I gave her a bottle of **tonic** water. You could say that I **Schweppe**d her off her feet.

Q: What do you call a Satanist who only eats low-carb **pizza**?

A: The Anti-**crust**.

.... ➤ ....

The owners of a restaurant were designing a new menu that included a lot of soups. They realized that they were going to have to start sourcing new ingredients for the menu.

"Where can we buy **chicken broth** in bulk?" one of them asked.

The other replied quickly, "The **stock** market."

.... ➤ ....

Q: What do you call a **turkey** that's come back to haunt you?

A: A **poultry**geist.

.... ➤ ....

My kids keep telling me to stop pretending to be **butter**, but I'm **on a roll** now!

Q: What does an annoying **pepper** do?

A: It gets **jalapeño** face.

. . . . ➤ . . . .

My partner is on a **tropical** food diet, and there is no other food in the house. It's enough to make a **mango** crazy.

. . . . ➤ . . . .

"Mom and I got stuck in a traffic **jam**."

"I hope you had **peanut butter** too."

. . . . ➤ . . . .

I'm on a **seafood** diet. I **see food** and I eat it.

. . . . ➤ . . . .

Steak puns are a **rare medium well done**.

I got caught stealing a pair of steaks from the supermarket last week.

The security guard stopped me and asked, "Now what do you think you are doing with that?"

I replied, "Well, I think potatoes and mushrooms would go nicely."

.... ➤ ....

Q: What do you call a line of people **lifting mozzarella**?

A: A **cheesy pickup** line.

.... ➤ ....

My dad and I were driving the car when we passed a sign for something called the **Peanut** Museum.

"Hey, Dad, do you want to stop there and have a look around?" I asked, pointing at the sign.

He shook his head and said, "No. I've heard that place is **nuts**."

I cut my finger while I was **chopping cheese**, but I think that I may have **grater** problems.

.... ➤ ....

The success or failure of a **pizza** joke is all in the **delivery**.

.... ➤ ....

"Dad, wouldn't it be fun if we made our own **butter**?"

"But won't that take an e**churn**ity?"

.... ➤ ....

Q: What do you call it when a hen looks at her salad?
A: Chicken **Caesar** salad.

My friend has changed so much since she decided to become a **vegan**. Sometimes, it's like I've never met **herbivore**.

Q: What do you feed a **zombie** who is a vegetarian?
A: GRAAAAAINS!

Did you hear about the town that had a big **molasses** spill? It sounded like a **sticky** situation.

Q: What did the **fried rice** say to the shrimp?
A: "Don't **wok** away from me!"

I was looking in the mirror yesterday, admiring my six-pack. Then I took it back to the kitchen and put it in the fridge.

Q: Why did the tomato **blush**?
A: It saw the salad **dressing**.

Milk is the fastest liquid on earth. It's **pasteurized** before you even see it!

. . . . ⚡ . . . .

Q: What do the people buying **pizza** have in common with the people selling it?
A: They both want each other's **dough**.

. . . . ⚡ . . . .

Just**ice** is a dish best served cold. Otherwise, you end up with just**water**.

. . . . ⚡ . . . .

Q: What's the most **dangerous** variety of cheese?
A: Sharp cheddar.

. . . . ⚡ . . . .

I don't like to argue about **Indian** food. You could say I'm **naan**-confrontational.

I tried to visit my favorite bar, but a sign on the door said it was closed for repairs. The next time I went in, I asked the bartender what the repair work had been about.

"Oh," he said. "One of the shelves that holds our spirits collapsed. Lots of broken glass."

"That's too bad," I told him. "I guess that shelf couldn't hold its liquor."

Did you hear about the guy who made a fortune investing in **Apple**? Turns out it was in **cider** trading.

Q: What did the **tomato** say to his friends when he was running late?
A: "Don't worry, I'll **ketchup**."

I would avoid **sushi** if I were you. It's a little bit **fishy**.

I'm a butcher, and a friend of mine is vegan. Usually, we're on good terms, but last time we saw each other, we got into a shouting match.

"People who sell meat are **disgusting**!" she yelled at me.

Luckily, I had the perfect retort. I said, "People who sell fruits and vegetables are **groc**er!"

D-LIST ENTERTAINMENT

I was browsing through the thrift store once when I came upon an old antique radio. The card on it said "For sale $1. Stuck at **max volume**."

I thought to myself, "Well, there's a deal I just **can't turn down**."

....

Q: Why does **Waldo** wear a striped shirt?

A: Because he doesn't want to be **spotted**.

I got hired as a security guard, and my boss told me that it was my job to watch **the office**. I'm on **season eight**, and I still can't figure out what this has to do with security.

Q: What kind of computer can **sing** really well?
A: A Dell.

"Dad, what do you want for your birthday this year?"

"Well, just **for the record**, I need a new **turntable**."

Q: What do you call a **rock-climbing** band of pirates?
A: The pirates of the **carabiners**.

I was watching a movie on my computer, but my **cat** kept stopping it. I guess she found the **paws** button.

.... ➤ ....

Q: Why do vampires steer clear of **Taylor Swift**?
A: She has **bad blood**.

.... ➤ ....

I was driving in the car with my dad on the weekend when an old, familiar song came on the radio. I couldn't quite place what it was.

"Is this Green Day?" I asked him.

He replied, "No. It's Sunday!"

.... ➤ ....

Q: What do you call Darth Vader when he's **nervous**?
A: **Panakin** Skywalker.

There are lots of books I want to read, but I just keep re-reading The Lord of the Rings over and over again. I think it's force of **hobbit**.

Q: What is E.T. short for?
A: He's got little legs.

"Dad, can we listen to the Beatles **today**?"

"No, but we can listen to the Beatles' '**Yesterday**.'"

Q: What do Winnie the Pooh, Alexander the Great, and Ivan the Terrible have in common?
A: They all have the same middle name.

I'm the **Norse god** of mischief, but I don't like to talk about it. I guess you could say I'm **Loki**.

Q: What is **Forrest Gump**'s password?
A: 1Forrest1.

. . . .

Accordion to a recent survey, inserting musical **instruments** randomly into sentences often goes unnoticed.

. . . .

Q: What superhero is the **best dressed**?
A: **Iron** Man.

. . . .

"Dad, can I watch the TV?"

"Sure, as long as you don't turn it on."

Q: How many **ears** does Captain Kirk have?

A: Three: the left ear, the right ear, and the final front**ier**.

.... → ....

Did you hear about **U2**'s lawyer? I hear he works pro **Bono**.

.... → ....

Q: What's made of **brass** and sounds like Tom Jones?

A: **Trombones**.

.... → ....

Q: Where does **Batman** go to the bathroom?

A: The **bat**room.

.... → ....

Have you heard about this new **music** group Cellophane? They mostly w**rap**.

Q: What do you call a group of **whales** playing instruments?

A: An **orca**stra.

· ⚡ ·

Marvel should try putting **advertisements** on the Hulk. He's a giant **Banner**.

· ⚡ ·

Q: What's the title of the upcoming Arnold Schwarzenegger movie about **classical music**?

A: *I'll Be* ***Bach***.

· ⚡ ·

Q: What did the **drummer** name his three daughters?

A: Anna 1, Anna 2, Anna 1 2 3 4.

A man was on trial for stealing dozens of guitars from different music shops around town. At the man's arraignment, the judge looked down at the guitar thief and asked him about his criminal history.

"First of**fender**?" the judge asked.

"No," the man replied sadly. "First a Gibson. Then a **Fender**."

· ➤ ·

When Jay-Z got **engaged** to his wife, did he call her his **Fiyoncé**?

· ➤ ·

Q: Why doesn't Ed have a **girlfriend** anymore?
A: Sheeran.

· ➤ ·

Q: What do you call a **potato** that makes internet videos?
A: A You**Tuber**.

Q: If all the superheroes started a **baseball** team, who would hit the most home runs?
A: Batman.

I'd just gone on a first date with a girl I really liked and was eager to tell my best friend about it.

"We went to a movie," I told him. "It was great."

"Awesome," he said. "Where did you meet?"

"Oh," I replied, confused that he couldn't figure it out. "Outside the movie theater, of course."

· ⚡ ·

Q: What was Beethoven's favorite **fruit**?
A: Ba-na-na-na, **ba-na-na**-na.

· ⚡ ·

If I were a **trumpet** player, I'd always borrow other people's trumpets. I hate to toot my own **horn**.

· ⚡ ·

Q: What did Darth Vader say when his car broke down three miles outside of town?
A: "The empire **hikes** back."

I asked my friend **Sam** to sing a song about smartphones the other day. **Sam**sung.

.... ➤ ....

Q: Who does Dorothy call when she's hankering for a glass of **juice**?
A: The Wizard of **OJ**.

.... ➤ ....

"Let's watch two episodes **back to back**."

"As long as I get to be the one **facing** the TV."

.... ➤ ....

A new study indicates that listening to albums by the band **Queen** might be bad for your health. They have a high **Mercury** content.

I took my family to a national park the other day. After I parked the car at the trailhead, a ranger approached us and asked if we had left any food in the car.

"We've got a lot of bears around here, and they'll try to get into cars if they smell food," the ranger said. "They'll even go for w**rappers**."

"Interesting," I said. "I didn't know bears liked **hip-hop**."

THE STEM OF BAD HUMOR

Over 5/4 of all people admit they are bad with fractions.

Did you ever hear the one about the **low-energy** laser? I guess you could say he was just **lazy**.

Q: How do you **eat** a computer?
A: Take a mega**byte**.

The best angle from which to approach any **problem** is the **try**angle.

If I see a robbery in an **Apple** Store, does that make me an **iWitness**?

Q: Why did the **zero** join the church?
A: She was already a **none**.

I don't know about you, but I find pressing **F5** **refreshing**.

I didn't want to take a class about **electricity**, but I just couldn't **resist**.

Q: Who built King Arthur's fabled **round** table?
A: **Sir Cumference**.

.... ➤ ....

Parallel lines have so much in common. It's a shame they'll **never meet**.

.... ➤ ....

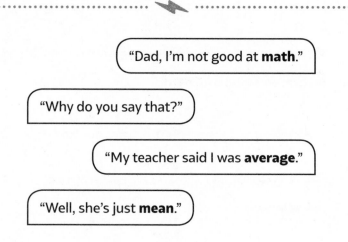

"Dad, I'm not good at **math**."

"Why do you say that?"

"My teacher said I was **average**."

"Well, she's just **mean**."

.... ➤ ....

My phone lost all its **contacts**, so I bought it a pair of **glasses** instead.

I, for one, like **Roman numerals**.

Q: Why is six afraid of seven?
A: It's not; numbers aren't sentient and can't feel fear.

When **Mile**y Cyrus goes to Europe, do they call her **Kilometer**y Cyrus?

Anyone can understand the Fibonacci sequence. It's as easy as 0, 1, 1, 2, 3.

Q: What did the 0 say to the 8?
A: "Nice **belt**."

There is a short line between numerators and denominators.

"Dad, I need a new computer **mic** to record audio."

"Why not a computer **Tom** or a computer **Jim** instead?"

My wife asked me to **sync** her iPhone, so I dropped it in the **lake**. I don't see what she's so upset about.

I tried to visit a weight loss **website**, but they require you to have **cookies** disabled.

Q: What do you call a **fish** made up of two sodium atoms?
A: Two Na.

I used to get small **shocks** every time I touched metal objects, but I don't anymore. I'm ex-**static**.

I make bad **science** puns, but only **periodic**ally.

Q: What do you call the **dog** that helps a scientist with his science experiments?
A: A **lab** assistant.

When I was in high school, I liked to clown around a lot. Once, my science teacher was explaining the nuances of **atomic structure**. I listened for a while, then raised my hand.

I told him, "You **Bohr** me."

Q: What is the **smartest** cell in the body?
A: A **STEM** cell.

The **circle** is the most ridiculous shape in the world. There's **no point** to it!

Want to hear a **science** joke? Never mind. It doesn't **matter**.

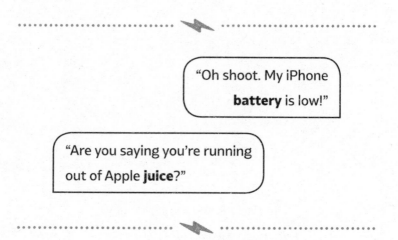

"Oh shoot. My iPhone **battery** is low!"

"Are you saying you're running out of Apple **juice**?"

My ex-girlfriend was obsessed with trying to find the **largest** known prime number. I wonder what she's **up to** now.

GROAN FOR THE GOAL

I thought up a great joke about **boxing** last night, but I forgot the **punch**line.

· ⚡ ·

Dodger Stadium is the largest **baseball stadium** in the United States by capacity. They say it can hold up to fifty-six thousand people. But that's just a **ballpark** figure.

Q: Why don't they let players wear **glasses** in football?
A: It's a **contact** sport.

.... ➤ ....

I asked my date to meet me at the **gym**, but she never showed up. I guess the two of us aren't going to **work out**.

.... ➤ ....

Winter sports fans need to accept it: **skiing** is going **downhill**.

.... ➤ ....

Q: Which Olympic sport generates the most **conversation**?
A: **Discus**.

My daughter is dating a **soccer player**. I was skeptical at first, as dads are about their daughters' boyfriends. After spending some time with him though, I had to hand it to her; he is a **keeper**.

· ⚡ ·

Some people say **NASCAR** is boring, but those people are just **race**-ist.

· ⚡ ·

Q: What's the most common sports injury for a **pig**?
A: A pulled **ham**string.

· ⚡ ·

I'm thinking about buying a **fitness** tracker. I'll need one in the **long run**.

After dinner, my partner asked me if I could **clear** the table. I was a **hurdler** in high school, so I managed it no problem.

Q: Why isn't **suntanning** an Olympic sport?
A: You can only get **bronze**.

.... ➤ ....

I got my son an autographed **baseball glove** from his favorite player for his birthday. He couldn't believe it was real, but I told him it was legit a **mitt**.

.... ➤ ....

"Dad, I really like **bad**minton, and I think I want to join a badminton club."

"What do you have against **good**minton?"

.... ➤ ....

You've got to love the camaraderie of **soccer**. The players are all working toward one common **goal**.

Golf is the only sport where sub**par** performance is ideal.

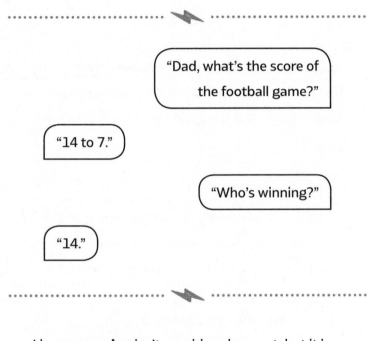

"Dad, what's the score of the football game?"

"14 to 7."

"Who's winning?"

"14."

I know **camping** isn't considered a sport, but it is in **tents**.

I thought about pursuing **archery**, but there are just too many **drawbacks**.

I work at a **sporting goods** store, but I think I'm going to quit to photograph carp wearing clothes. It will be called **Shooting Fish in Apparel**.

Q: Why did the baseball player have to be treated for **rabies**?
A: He was around **bats** all the time.

I thought I had a good joke about **yoga**, but it was a bit of a **stretch**.

After the fundraising event, the kids on the **baseball** team were supposed to help clean up, but I could see right off the **bat** that they weren't going to **pitch** in.

"What are you doing in gym class these days?"

"We're learning how to play **tennis**."

"How do you like it? Are you getting into the **swing** of things?"

····· ⚡ ·····

I've never played **paintball** before, but I decided to give it a **shot**!

····· ⚡ ·····

I was playing with a **boomerang** and couldn't remember how to use it. Then it **came back** to me.

····· ⚡ ·····

Q: What did the **mountain** climber name his son?
A: Cliff.

Q: Can a shoe **box**?

A: No, but a tin can!

The Russian member of my human pyramid team recently moved away. Now we don't have O**leg** to **stand** on.

· ⚡ ·

I like **soccer**, but I'm not trying to go pro. I just do it for **kicks**.

· ⚡ ·

Q: Why did the stadium get **hot** after the game?
A: All the **fans** left.

· ⚡ ·

Say what you want about **gymnasts**, but they really **bend over backward** for their country.

· ⚡ ·

I tried to date a **tennis** player once, but **love** meant nothing to her.

We were watching the Olympics, and one of the **relay** races was on. My son was confused about what was going on.

"What's a relay race?" he asked.

I explained to him how relay races work and how the **baton** is used. He understood it right away. I have to **hand it** to him.

• ➤ •

There are always winners and **lugers** in the **Winter Olympics**.

• ➤ •

Q: How do **vegetables** cheer for their teammates?

A: By **root**ing for them!

• ➤ •

Did you read about the **jockey** who got arrested for attacking other riders? They charged him with excessive use of **horse**.

"Dad, do you want a **box** for your leftovers?"

"No, but I'll **wrestle** you for them!"

· ⚡ ·

I can't decide if I like **baseball**. It's really **hit** or **miss**.

WORKPLACE WISECRACKS

I heard there's no training to be a **trash collector**. You just **pick it up** as you go along.

······························· ➤ ·····························

Did you hear about the **lumberjack** who got fired for cutting down too many trees? He **saw** too much.

······························· ➤ ·····························

Q: Why do secret agents get the best **sleep**?
A: Because they're always under**cover**.

I passed a **cabinet** maker's truck, and the side said "**Counter** Fitters."

· ⚡ ·

My husband and I got a call from the police today.

"I'm sorry to have to tell you this," the officer said. "But your son is wanted for questioning about a fire in the area."

I couldn't believe it.

"Was it ar**son**?" my husband asked.

"Yes," said the officer. "It was **your son**."

· ⚡ ·

If you make v**log**s, does that make you a v**lumberjack**?

· ⚡ ·

If you are trying to get a job in the moisturizer industry, the best advice I can give is to **apply daily**.

· ⚡ ·

My job is top secret. Even I don't know what I'm doing.

My friend wrote an autobiography. He decided to bind the books himself, but he says he accidentally **glued** himself to one of the books. That's his story, and he's **sticking** to it.

Q: How did the **astronaut** break up with his girlfriend?
A: He told her he just needed **space**.

"Dad, why do scuba divers roll backward off boats?"

"Because if they rolled forward, they'd still be in the boat."

Did you hear about the **actor** who fell through the floorboards? He was just going through a **stage**.

I always wanted to be a **Gregorian** monk, but I never got the **chants**.

• ➤ •

Today, I used the **elevator** to get up to my office rather than taking the stairs. It was an up**lifting** experience.

• ➤ •

My boss stopped by the office this morning to ask about the project I was working on. After a few minutes, she said she had to go to a meeting and walked away. Before she left, she told me to have a good day. So I went home!

• ➤ •

I read an article today about a guy who became an **ax** murderer after his failed career as a comedian. In both cases, he was a total **hack**.

• ➤ •

Never invite a **carpenter** to a party. He'll just get **hammer**ed.

Q: What's a chef's **first job** after finishing culinary school?

A: Finding an **entrée**-level position.

.... 🔗 ....

In college, I worked to construct and pave a **cul-de-sac**. It was a **dead-end** job.

.... 🔗 ....

I met a **taxidermist** who wasn't very talkative. I asked him what he did for a living, and he just said, "**Stuff**."

.... 🔗 ....

A military sergeant was talking with his commanding officer.

"I didn't see you at camouflage training this morning, Sergeant," the major said.

The sergeant smiled and responded, "Thank you, sir!"

.... 🔗 ....

You can't ever trust a **merchant**. They're such **traders**.

My boss needed me to hang a picture frame and said I could use a **ladder** or a lift. I chose the **latter**.

I was at a **coffee** shop getting my morning coffee, and one of the employees had a meltdown, quitting her job right on the spot. I guess she was tired of the same old **grind**.

· ➤ ·

I had a job as a **telemarketer** once, but I got fired. My boss told me I'd been **phoning** it in.

· ➤ ·

I applied for a new job last week. When they brought me in for an interview, the hiring manager seemed very interested in my work schedule.

"So, you currently work nine to five, Monday through Friday?" she asked.

"Yes, ma'am," I replied.

"Would you be willing to work outside those hours?" she asked.

"No," I said. "I'd rather not catch a cold."

Astronauts are such snobs. They **look down** on everyone.

· ⟫ ·

Q: What are **bald** sea captains most worried about?
A: Capsizes.

· ⟫ ·

A police officer caught two kids misbehaving. One was playing with a **firework**, and the other was playing with a car **battery**. The police officer **charged** one and **let off** the other one.

· ⟫ ·

I'm a **lawyer**, and my wife and I got in a fight recently because she was fed up with my very particular brand of humor.

"The jokes were funny at first," she said. "But they're getting old! All you do is make **courthouse** puns!"

"**Guilty**," I said.

Q: What do you call a **factory** that manufactures products that are just passable?
A: A satis**factory**.

• ⚡ •

The **invisible** man turned down a fantastic job offer. He just couldn't **see** himself doing it.

• ⚡ •

I used to work at a **calendar** factory, but I got fired after I took a couple of **days** off.

• ⚡ •

Q: What kind of shoes do **ninjas** wear?
A: **Sneak**ers.

• ⚡ •

My old job involved crushing **cans**. I had to quit because it was **soda**-pressing.

They laughed when I said I wanted to be a comedian, but nobody's laughing now!

.... ➤ ....

Q: What do you call someone whose job it is to separate fact from fiction?
A: A librarian.

.... ➤ ....

I recently got a job working at a toy factory. I work in the Halloween action figure department, where two of us work on the production line for **Dracula** figures. It's demanding work. I have to make every second **count**.

.... ➤ ....

Repairing **elevators** is tough work, so you'd think those guys would be well paid. In reality, they really get the **shaft**.

Q: How did the **librarian** run so fast?
A: She knew how to **book** it.

.... ➤ ....

I read about a **cartoonist** who went missing.
Details are **sketch**y at this time.

.... ➤ ....

I used to have a job **digging** tunnels underground.
It was really **boring**.

.... ➤ ....

I start my new job at a **restaurant** tomorrow. I
can't **wait**.

.... ➤ ....

Q: How does an **undertaker** make his money?
A: He **urns** it.

At the bar a few days ago, I got into a conversation with a **lumberjack**. He was telling me about his profession, which I found fascinating. At one point, he mentioned that he has cut down exactly 3,384 trees over the course of his career. I asked how he could possibly know the precise number.

"Oh," he replied matter-of-factly. "I always keep a **log**."

. . . . ⚡ . . . .

I just started a new job with lots of great benefits. When I told my wife about all the perks, she asked if there was a **gym** in the building.

"I don't know," I said. "I haven't met **everybody** yet."

. . . . ⚡ . . . .

I never thought my brother would try to steal my job as a **road worker**. Then I started seeing the **signs**.

. . . . ⚡ . . . .

I just interviewed for a **waiter** job at my favorite restaurant. I hope they saw that I could bring a lot to the **table.**

I started a **roofing** business, but
I keep losing money on projects.
I think it's because I keep
building them **on the house**.

I work on a **submarine**, but I think I'm going to quit. I'm under a lot of **pressure**.

.... ➤ ....

Q: What's the difference between an angry circus owner and a Roman barber?
A: One is a raving showman, the other is a shaving Roman.

.... ➤ ....

I went to see a **mime** improvisation show the other day, and the performance was spectacular. It goes **without saying**.

.... ➤ ....

I hired a few construction workers to come out and remove the asbestos from my attic. They came to my house three times with different tools but said they couldn't get all of it. I guess they tried as**best**os they could.

ARE WE THERE YET?

A friend of mine sued an airline for losing his **luggage**. He ultimately won the lawsuit but still lost his **case**.

It might not be safe for me to drive this car right now, but bad **brakes** have never **stopped** me before.

Q: What is a **missionary**'s favorite car?
A: A **convert**ible.

There was an inspirational song playing in the car that kept telling me to go the extra mile. Now I'm out of gas, and I don't know where I am.

I have a fear of **speed bumps**, but I'm slowly **getting over** it.

Q: What kind of bagel can **fly**?
A: A **plain** bagel.

I have a joke about a flat **tire**, but I'll **spare** you from it.

I don't want to **bike** anymore. It's **two tires**ome.

The **flight** was easy enough, but the food wasn't great. It was very **plane**.

· ⚡ ·

Q: What do you do if you see **a space**man?
A: Park your car, man.

· ⚡ ·

I got caught sneaking onto a train once. I told the security guard that the **price** wasn't **fare**.

· ⚡ ·

I was teaching my daughter how to drive today. We climbed into the car, and she asked what she should do first.

"Well, put the key in the ignition and start the car," I said. "Then shift into **reverse** to get us out of the garage."

She followed the instructions perfectly, and soon we were reversing out of the garage.

"Ah, this **takes me back**," I told her.

You can turn any boat into a **hat**. Just turn it over and it's **cap**sized.

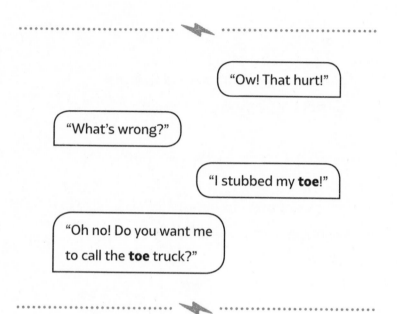

"Ow! That hurt!"

"What's wrong?"

"I stubbed my **toe**!"

"Oh no! Do you want me to call the **toe** truck?"

Did you hear that **train** that just went by? It left **tracks**.

Q: What's the fastest speed that people can **board an airplane**?
A: Terminal velocity.

Apparently, I snore too loud. It scared everyone in the car I was driving.

Two **fish** are in a **tank**. One turns to the other and says, "Hey, how do we drive this thing?"

Q: What do you call a boat that's **50 percent off**?
A: A **sale** boat.

My wife and I decided it would be fun to take a day off work and go kayaking. Once we got to the launch site and got the boat in the water, my wife handed me two kayak **paddles**.

"Which one do you want?" she asked.

"Oh," I said. "I'll take either **oar**."

I tried to woo a girl at a party with my extensive knowledge of the *Titanic*, but she didn't seem interested. I guess it wasn't a good **icebreaker**.

Q: What do you call an airplane that flies **backward**?
A: A **receding** airline.

My wife likes to bike to work. Unfortunately, during part of the year, that means she's biking in the dark. We recently bought her a helmet lamp so that she can see where she's going on dark mornings. The drawback is that she doesn't love how it looks.

"I look like a **miner**," she said after putting it on for the first time.

"No way!" I said. "You definitely look at least **thirty-five**."

My sister bet me that I couldn't build a car out of **spaghetti**. You should have seen her face as I drove **pasta**.

They used to charge you a quarter to **fill up your car tires with air**. Now they charge $1.50. That's what I call **inflation**.

· ⚡ ·

"Dad, can I wash the car with you?"

"I don't know, Son. I'd prefer you use a sponge."

· ⚡ ·

Q: What kind of car does an **egg** drive?
A: A **Yolk**swagen.

· ⚡ ·

One of my favorite memories from childhood is my dad rolling us down the hill in old **car tires**. Those were the **Goodyears**.

I read in the newspaper that a **red** ship and a **blue** ship had collided in the Caribbean. The article said that the survivors were **maroon**ed.

············· ⚡ ·············

My wife gave birth to our **son** in the **car** on the way to the hospital. We named him **Carson**.

············· ⚡ ·············

Q: What did the car say when it got **hurt**?
A: "**Au**di."

············· ⚡ ·············

"Dad, I'd love to learn more about buoyancy."

"Whatever floats your boat."

Q: What did the bumper sticker on the **trailer** say?

A: "I go where I'm **towed**."

Q: What sound does a **747** make when it bounces?
A: Boeing, Boeing.

I couldn't find my ice scraper in my car, so I used a grocery store **discount** card instead. It only got **20 percent off**.

I started a business building **boats** in my attic. Let me tell you: **sails** are going through the roof.

When I fly, I like to hang **air fresheners** in the plane. It helps with de**scent**.

Q: What do you call a Subaru covered in road **salt**?
A: An Im**pretzel**.

I built a car out of my old **sports clothes**. You could say it runs **Lycra** dream.

· ↘ ·

My husband told me that I had no sense of **direction**. It made me so mad that I packed up and **right**.

· ↘ ·

Q: What's the difference between a well-dressed man on a **unicycle** and a poorly dressed man on a **bicycle**? **A:** At**tire**.

· ↘ ·

I tried to imagine the Titanic with a lisp, but it was **unthinkable**.

· ↘ ·

I didn't want my wife to know that I was playing with my son's **train** set, so I threw a sheet over it to cover my **tracks**.

WHAT THE DOCTOR ORDERED

I accidentally swallowed some **food coloring**. The doctor says I'm okay, but I feel like I'm **dying** inside.

Last night, my wife woke me up in the middle of the night to tell me she was in labor. Quickly, I called an ambulance to take us to the hospital.

"Okay, sir. It's going to be all right," the woman on the phone said. "Is this your wife's first baby?"

I replied, "No, this is her husband!"

I was making dinner once when I accidentally cut my hand badly. I had to go to the hospital to get stitches. Once the doctor was done stitching me up, I asked him the question I had on my mind.

"When this heals, will I be able to play guitar?" I asked.

The doctor smiled. "Of course," he said. "You'll be just fine in a few days."

I was elated. "Awesome! I've always wanted to play an instrument."

· ➤ ·

One time, I went to a party with a bunch of **anesthesiologists**. It was a **gas**!

· ➤ ·

I fell halfway out the **window** last week. I went to the doctor, but I've been in **pane** ever since.

· ➤ ·

Nurses who give people **shots** all the time must be sad. Their jobs are **in vein**.

Q: What do you call a **mummy** with a cold?
A: Sir Cough, I guess.

A couple of years ago, my doctor told me I was going **deaf**. I haven't **heard** from him since.

"Dad, what's my blood type?"

"Red."

I was genuinely shocked when my doctor told me I was **colorblind**. It came out of the **purple**!

Q: What's red and bad for your teeth?
A: A brick.

Mary had a little lamb. The doctor fainted.

• ⚡ • • • • • • • • • • • • • • • • • •

I was walking through the park last week and saw a man on roller skates going around the path. He was going really fast. I'm not sure what happened, but he tripped and fell hard on the pavement. I ran over to him to see if he was okay. He looked like he was in pain.

"I think I broke my arm!" he told me. "Would you do me a favor and call me a doctor?"

I gave him a dubious look. "I don't see how it will help," I said. "But okay. You're a doctor."

• ⚡ • • • • • • • • • • • • • • • • • •

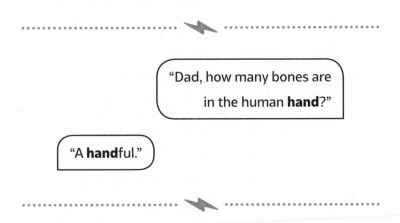

"Dad, how many bones are in the human **hand**?"

"A **hand**ful."

• ⚡ • • • • • • • • • • • • • • • • • •

I dis**located** my arm yesterday. Luckily, I **found** it again.

I saw a sad news bulletin that said that the inventor of the **cough** drop had passed away. There will be no **coffin** at their funeral.

....   ⟶   ....

Q: How did the **kleptomaniac** treat his condition?
A: He **took something** for it.

....   ⟶   ....

I went to the doctor's office for my annual checkup. They were running a little behind, so my appointment started fifteen minutes late. When the nurse came to get me in the waiting room, she was apologetic.

"I'm sorry for the wait," she said.

"Oh, that's okay," I told her. "I'm **patient**."

....   ⟶   ....

I'm going to talk to a surgeon about removing my **spine**. It's only holding me **back**.

"Dad, I have such bad heartburn, it feels like I ate a bunch of red ants."

"Maybe you should take an **ant**acid."

Q: What do you call a mythical creature with a **cold**?
A: Achoopacabra.

I was going to get a **brain** transplant, but then I changed my **mind**.

Q: What do you call an Instagram star who has fallen **ill**?
A: An **influenza**.

My doctor wrote that I had type A **blood**, but he was wrong. Luckily, it was just a **type O**.

I hate when people make jokes about broken **arms**. They aren't **humerus**.

··· ➤ ···

A single, pregnant woman got into a car accident and went into a coma. Six months later, she woke up, and the first thing she did was ask the doctor about her baby.

"Babies," the doctor corrected her. "You gave birth to twins, a boy and a girl. They're both completely healthy. Your brother named them and is taking care of them."

"Oh no, not my brother!" the woman exclaimed. "He's a bit of an idiot. What did he name the girl?"

"Denise," the doctor answered.

The woman looked relieved. She said, "Oh, De**nise** isn't bad! What did he name the boy?"

The doctor replied, "De**nephew**."

··· ➤ ···

I'm not scared of most medical conditions, but I do know that if you come down with a **bladder** infection, **urine** trouble.